GOSPEL DUETS

8 INSPIRING HYMNS FOR ONE PIANO, FOUR HANDS

Arranged by Phillip Keveren

— PIANO LEVEL —
INTERMEDIATE

ISBN 978-1-5400-5532-3

Visit Hal Leonard Online at
www.halleonard.com

Visit Phillip at
www.phillipkeveren.com

Contact us:
Hal Leonard
7777 West Bluemound Road
Milwaukee, WI 53213
Email: info@halleonard.com

In Europe, contact:
Hal Leonard Europe Limited
42 Wigmore Street
Marylebone, London, W1U 2RN
Email: info@halleonardeurope.com

In Australia, contact:
Hal Leonard Australia Pty. Ltd.
4 Lentara Court
Cheltenham, Victoria, 3192 Australia
Email: info@halleonard.com.au

PREFACE

Playing duets is a great way for pianists to broaden their musical skills. This collaborative experience is important for musicians that spend a lot of practice time in isolation. Listening to another player to achieve blend and rhythmic precision is a rich, refining process.

The arrangements in this collection are of classic gospel hymns and songs that have stood the test of time. Each one has been sung, played, and hummed around the world for many decades. I hope these duets provide inspiration – whether in a recital, worship service or simple home setting – to both performers and listeners.

Sincerely,

Phillip Keveren

BIOGRAPHY

Phillip Keveren, a multi-talented keyboard artist and composer, has composed original works in a variety of genres from piano solo to symphonic orchestra. Mr. Keveren gives frequent concerts and workshops for teachers and their students in the United States, Canada, Europe, Australia, and Asia. He holds a B.M. in composition from California State University Northridge and a M.M. in composition from the University of Southern California.

CONTENTS

CHURCH IN THE WILDWOOD

Words and Music by DR. WILLIAM S. PITTS
Arranged by Phillip Keveren

HIS EYE IS ON THE SPARROW

Words by CIVILLA D. MARTIN
Music by CHARLES H. GABRIEL
Arranged by Phillip Keveren

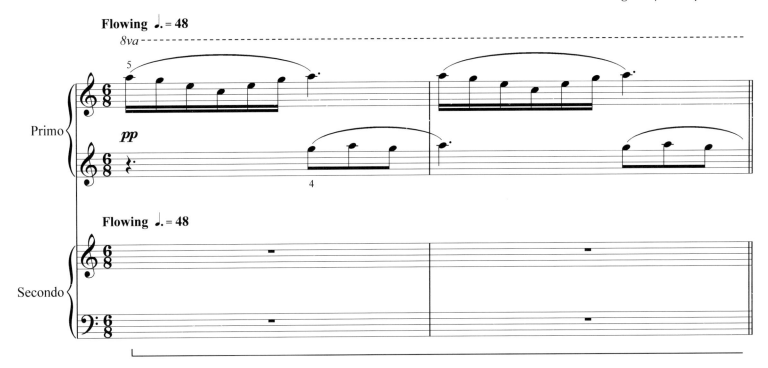

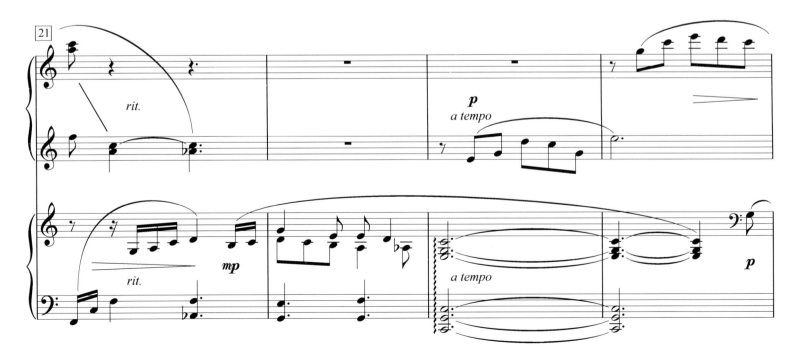

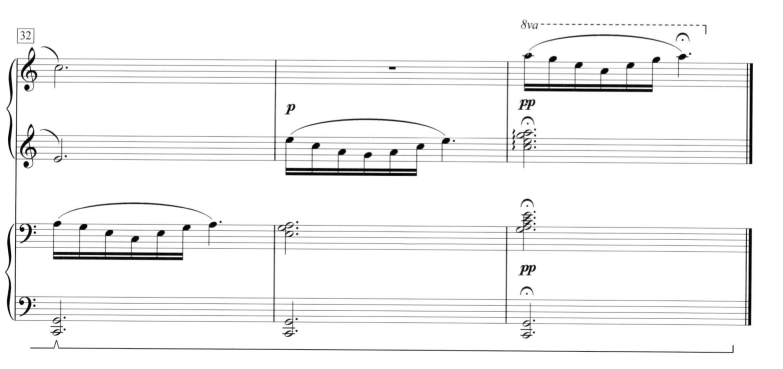

IN THE GARDEN

Words and Music by C. AUSTIN MILES
Arranged by Phillip Keveren

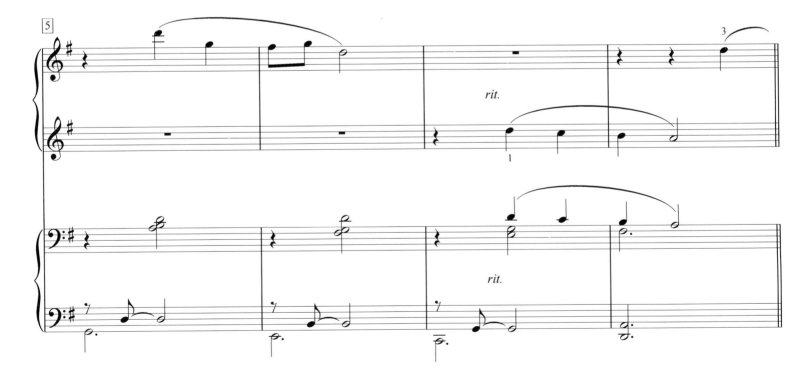

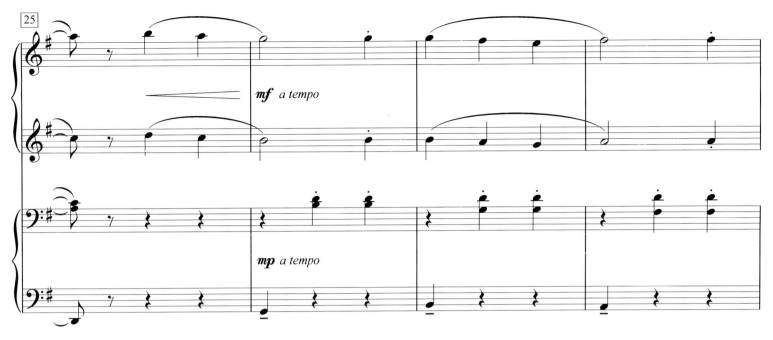

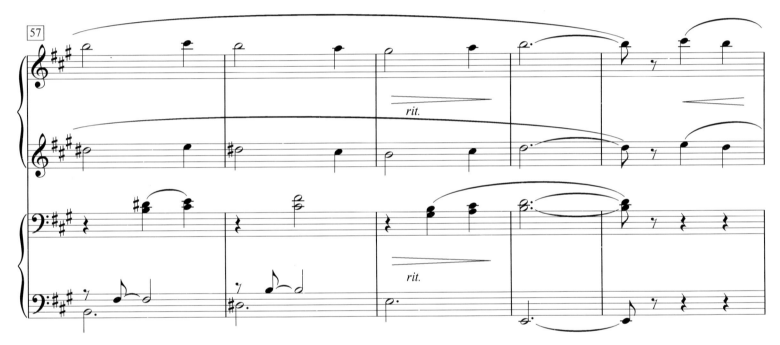

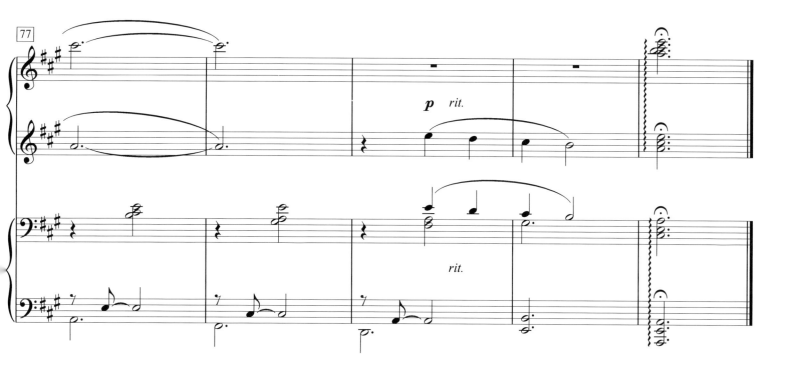

JUST A CLOSER WALK WITH THEE

Traditional
Arranged by KENNETH MORRIS
Arranged by Phillip Keveren

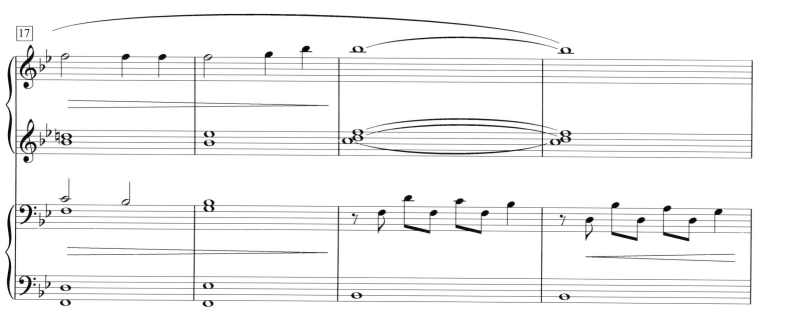

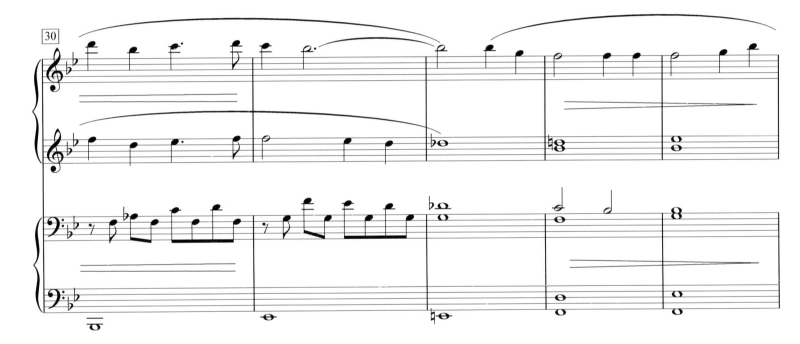

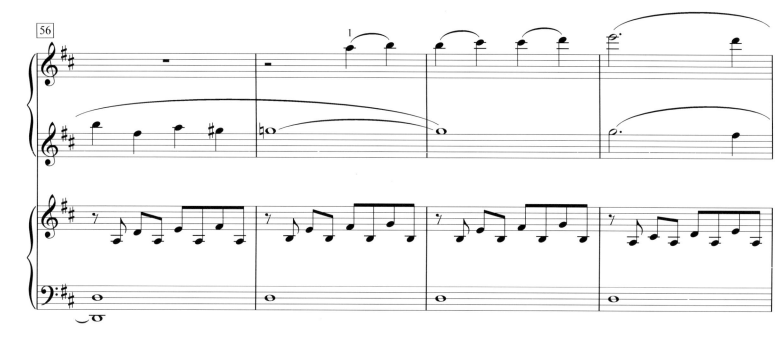

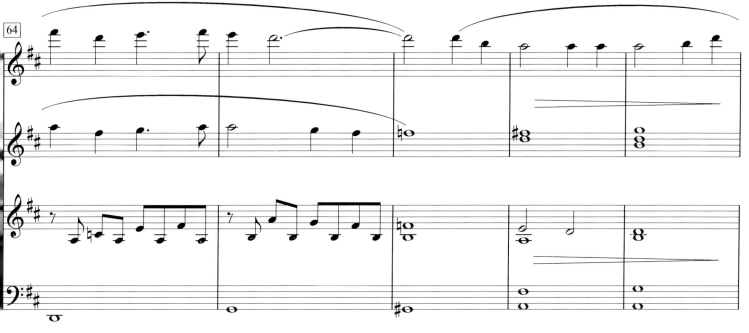

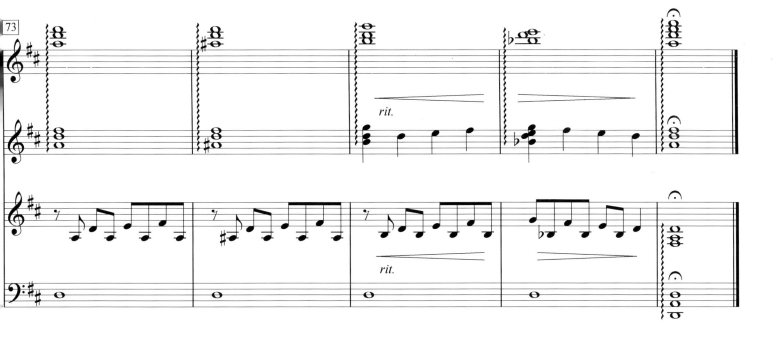

THE OLD RUGGED CROSS

Words and Music by REV. GEORGE BENNARD
Arranged by Phillip Keveren

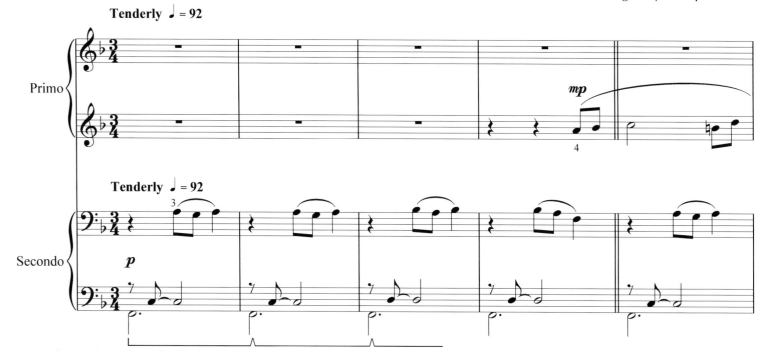

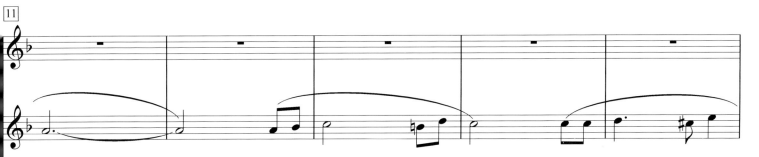

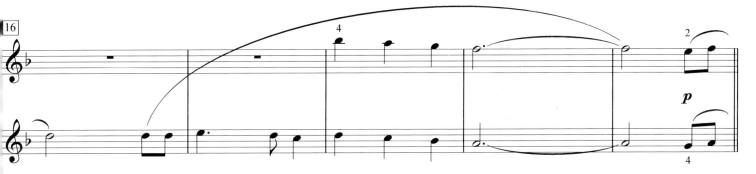

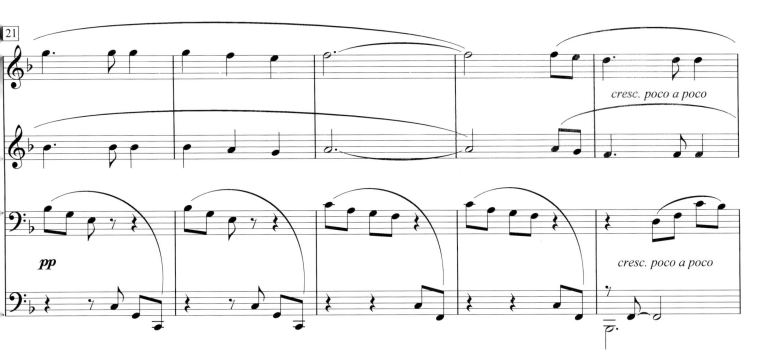

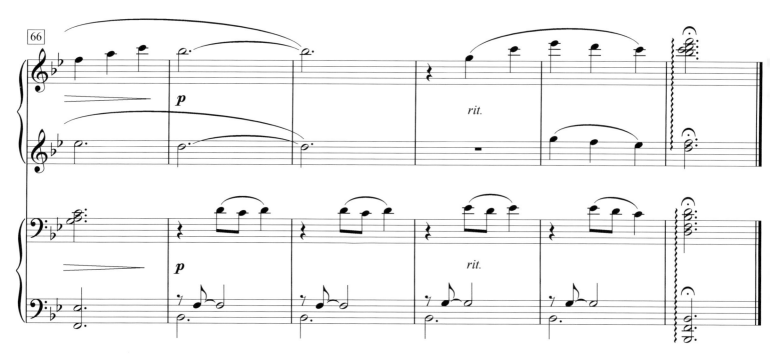

THERE IS POWER IN THE BLOOD

Words and Music by LEWIS E. JONES
Arranged by Phillip Keveren

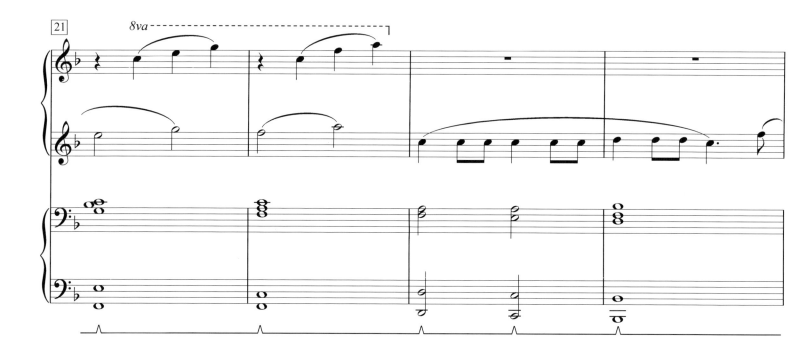

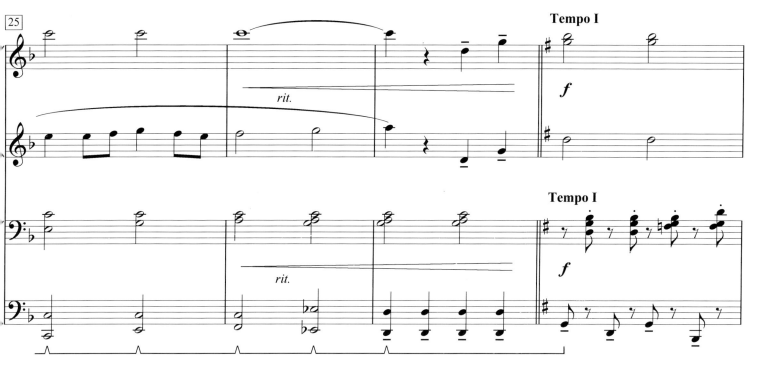

Tempo I

Tempo I

SHALL WE GATHER AT THE RIVER?

Words and Music by ROBERT LOWRY
Arranged by Phillip Keveren

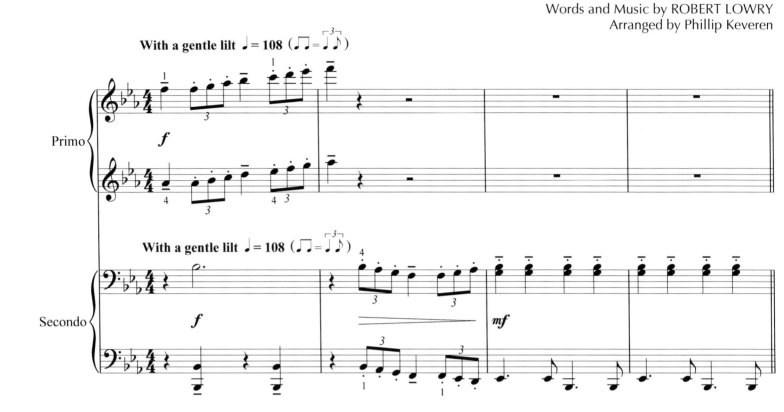

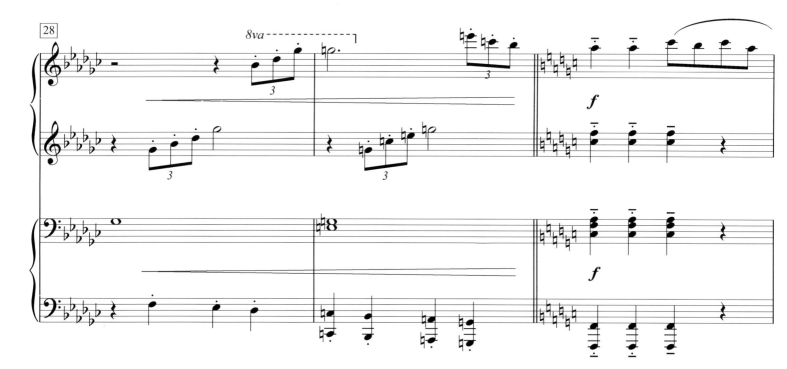

WHEN THE ROLL IS CALLED UP YONDER

Words and Music by JAMES M. BLACK
Arranged by Phillip Keveren

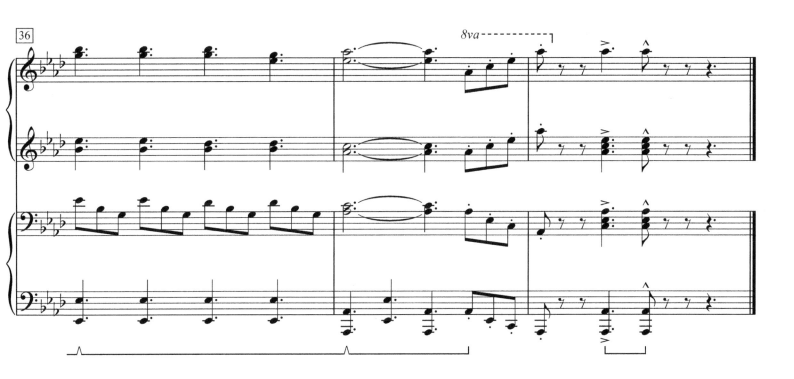